DATE DUE

JUL 0 1 1999		
OCT 0 3 2001		
MAY 3 0 2003		
SEP 2 4 2003		

HIGHSMITH 45-220

People to Know

Neil Armstrong

The First Man on the Moon

Barbara Kramer

Enslow Publishers, Inc.

44 Fadem Road   PO Box 38
Box 699   Aldershot
Springfield, NJ 07081   Hants GU12 6BP
USA   UK

Library of Congress Cataloging-in-Publication Data

Kramer, Barbara.
    Neil Armstrong : the first man on the moon / by Barbara Kramer.
      p. cm. — (People to know)
    Includes bibliographical references and index.
    Summary: Explores the life and accomplishments of astronaut Neil Armstrong,
from his childhood in Ohio through his years with NASA, including his famous
moon landing and other space flights.
    ISBN 0-89490-828-6
    1. Armstrong, Neil, 1930–   —Juvenile literature. 2. Astronauts—United
States—Biography—Juvenile literature. [1. Armstrong, Neil, 1930– .
2. Astronauts.] I. Title. II. Series.
TL789.85.A75K73   1997
629.45'0092—dc21
[B]

                                      96-45143
                                        CIP
                                          AC

Printed in the United States of America

10 9 8 7 6 5

Illustration Credits: Archive Photos, p. 99; National Aeronautics and Space
Administration (NASA), pp. 4, 9, 30, 35, 37, 44, 48, 53, 58, 61, 65, 69, 71,
79, 81, 83, 88, 91; Ohio Historical Society, pp. 15, 18, 27, 75; University of
Cincinnati, p. 93.

Cover Illustration: National Aeronautics and Space Administration (NASA).

Contents

Neil Armstrong

A Dream to Fly

On July 20, 1969, astronaut Neil Armstrong was a quarter of a million miles from earth. He had already spent three days in space, and the most dangerous part of his journey was about to begin.

Soon he would attempt the first landing on the moon in a strange-looking vehicle called a lunar module (LM). The LM looked more like a giant insect than a spacecraft. It had a boxlike cabin with thin aluminum sides that sat on top of four long, spidery legs.

It had an automated landing system, but Armstrong needed to be able to take control of the spacecraft in case of an emergency. For months, he had made practice lunar landings in a lunar landing research vehicle (LLRV). Although Armstrong had logged many hours in the LLRV, he knew there might be surprises when it came time for the actual lunar landing. The LM was designed to be flown in the moon's gravity field, which is about one-sixth as strong as the earth's gravity. It was impossible to duplicate those exact conditions on earth. In reality, this landing would be the test flight.

Danger was not new to Armstrong. He got his pilot's license when he was only sixteen years old, and during the Korean War (1950–1953) he served his country as a Navy fighter pilot. Later, he became a civilian test pilot flying experimental aircraft like the X-15 rocket plane to the fringes of space. He had been commander of the *Gemini 8* space mission in 1966. Now he was commander of the three-man *Apollo 11* crew. Armstrong had a reputation for keeping a cool head during an emergency. It was an ability that would help him now as he attempted to make the first lunar landing.

Michael Collins and Edwin E. Aldrin, Jr., completed the *Apollo 11* team. They were both experienced Air Force pilots, and they had both made previous space flights in 1966. On this mission, Collins was the pilot of the command module (CM). He would remain in the CM, continuing an orbit sixty-nine miles from the moon's surface while Armstrong and Aldrin made their descent to the moon in the LM.

Before the flight, code names had been assigned to the space vehicles. Those names were used in communications with Mission Control, which was located in the Manned Spacecraft Center (now called the

Johnson Space Center) in Houston, Texas. The CM was called *Columbia,* and the LM, *Eagle.* Armstrong and Aldrin were headed to a spot on the moon called the Sea of Tranquility.

Aldrin, who was known as "Buzz" to most of the astronauts, was the LM pilot. He crawled through a tunnel connecting the two space modules and began checking the power and the communications equipment in the LM. Armstrong joined him later.

At Mission Control, there was an astronaut named Charlie Duke who was the capcom, the capsule communicator, for the lunar landing. His job was to relay information from Mission Control to the astronauts and to get information from the astronauts. Two minutes before *Columbia* orbited behind the moon, Duke gave the astronauts a "go" from Mission Control for undocking.

Radio waves could not bend around the moon. That meant that the astronauts were out of contact with ground control when Collins threw a switch and the LM floated away from the CM.

As the vehicles emerged from the back side of the moon, radio contact was reestablished. Duke wanted a report on the undocking. "How does it look, Neil?" he asked.[1]

"The *Eagle* has wings," Armstrong answered.

The two vehicles flew close together at first. It gave Collins time to examine the LM. He had to make sure there were no problems that would interfere with the LM's flight.

When he was finished with his inspection, Collins gave Armstrong his report. "I think you've got a fine looking flying machine there, *Eagle*, despite the fact you're upside-down."

"Somebody's upside-down," Armstrong replied.

Actually, in space there is no up or down. However, in the first part of their flight, the two astronauts aboard the *Eagle* did appear to be turned around. The bottom of the LM was pointed toward the moon, and the astronauts were flying backward, leaning toward their controls, facing downward.

Collins fired small rockets on the CM to put some distance between it and the LM. "Okay, *Eagle*. . . . You guys take care," he said.

"See you later," Armstrong replied. They sounded as casual as two men headed home after an ordinary day at work.

As the LM orbited behind the moon again, the computer triggered the descent engine to fire. That began the LM's descent to the moon's surface.

"The burn was on time," Aldrin reported as they came into contact with Mission Control again. He read out the computer information on the firing, or "burn." Mission Control concluded that, so far, their descent was looking good.

"You're GO for PDI . . . ," Duke radioed from Mission Control.

The initials PDI stood for powered descent initiation. It meant that the LM's rocket would begin one last continuous firing for a twelve-minute sweep to the moon's surface.

During the descent, the on-board computer commanded the control jets to fire, and the LM turned until the astronauts were standing upright facing the

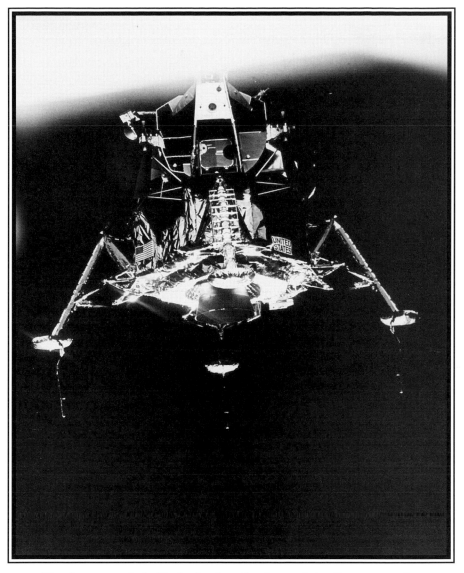

The lunar module Eagle *begins its descent to the moon after undocking from the command module* Columbia. *Astronaut Michael Collins took this photo from the window of* Columbia.

moon. There were no seats in the LM, and the astronauts had loose harnesses to hold them in place. They stood side by side at the controls much like trolley-car drivers as they approached their landing site.

Suddenly an alarm screeched. "PROGRAM ALARM," Armstrong called. "It's a 1202," he added.

At Mission Control, twenty-six-year-old Steve Bales studied the codes on his computer. He was the guidance officer on duty, and he was an expert on the LM's computer system. He understood the problem immediately. The spacecraft's computer was overloaded.

"Give us a reading on the 1202 PROGRAM ALARM," Armstrong urged.

The flight director, Gene Kranz, would decide what to do next. He was relying on Bales's expert opinion, and he needed an answer now. Should they continue the descent to the moon or abort?

Bales quickly thought through the situation. The computer was working, and he knew that it was set up to receive the most important information first. It should get all the data needed for the landing.

"Go!" he called to Kranz.[2]

"We got—we're GO on that alarm," the capcom, Charlie Duke, told the astronauts on the LM.

At three thousand feet, the alarm sounded again, and then at two thousand feet. Each time, the word from Mission Control was "Go."

Aldrin kept his eyes on the on-board computer, calling out the numbers: "Five hundred forty feet, down at—thirty." They were 540 feet from the surface of the moon and descending at a rate of thirty feet per second.

As they got closer to the moon's surface, Armstrong saw that the computer was taking them to a landing site that had many large boulders. It was critical that the LM land in a flat area so that it was in position to be launched from the moon.

At three hundred feet, Armstrong turned off the automated landing system. He would have to fly the *Eagle* manually to another landing spot.

"Seventy-five feet. . . . Down a half, six forward . . . ," Aldrin said.

"Sixty seconds," Duke announced. His words were a warning to the astronauts. The LM had only enough fuel left for sixty seconds of flying. If they ran out of fuel at this altitude, the LM would crash on the moon's surface before they had time to fire their ascent engine.

"Light's on," Aldrin reported. It was a flashing amber light signaling low fuel.

Aldrin continued chanting the computer readouts, "Down two and a half. Forward. Forward. . . . Forty feet, down two and a half. Kicking up some dust." The LM was close enough to stir up dust on the moon's surface.

Armstrong was silent, looking for a place to land. Tension was high at Mission Control as they waited.

"Thirty feet, two and a half down. Faint shadow. Four forward. Four forward. Drifting to the right a little . . ."

"Thirty seconds," Duke said, barely concealing the urgency in his voice.

"Contact light!" Aldrin called. The sensors on one of the LM's feet had touched the surface.

Aldrin continued his readouts: "Okay. ENGINE STOP."

From Mission Control, Duke radioed the astronauts, "We copy you down, *Eagle*."

"Houston, Tranquility Base here," Armstrong replied. There was a pause, and then he continued, "THE *EAGLE* HAS LANDED."

Cheering erupted at Mission Control.

"Roger, Tranquility," Duke said. "We copy you on the ground. You got a bunch of guys about to turn blue. We're breathing again. Thanks a lot."

Buzz Aldrin reached over to shake Armstrong's hand and saw a happy face grinning back at him.[3]

As a boy, Armstrong had a recurring dream that if he held his breath he could float up from his bed and hover above it. He later said that it was a frustrating dream because he never actually went anywhere. He was not content to hover. He wanted to fly.

Now he had landed on the moon. It had been a long journey beginning on August 5, 1930, when Neil Alden Armstrong was born in his grandparents' farmhouse about five miles outside Wapakoneta, Ohio.

A First Look at the Moon

Neil Armstrong's interest in flying began early. His parents, Stephen and Viola Armstrong, remembered taking him to the Cleveland Municipal Airport to watch the airplanes take off and land when he was only two years old. "He was so fascinated he was never ready to leave," his mother recalled.[1]

When Neil was three years old, his sister, June, was born. His brother, Dean, came along about eighteen months later.

Stephen Armstrong was an auditor of county records for the state of Ohio. His job was to go through county financial reports to make sure they were accurate. It took him about a year to examine a county's books. Then he started all over again in another county.

Because of his work, the family moved often, living in various cities and towns in Ohio such as Cleveland, Warren, and Jefferson. They lived in furnished apartments and houses so that when it was time to move, they did not have to bother hauling furniture. They packed everything they owned into their car and drove to the next county.

Viola Armstrong was a full-time homemaker who enjoyed literature and music. They were interests her older son, Neil, also acquired. By the time he started school, Neil already knew how to read. As a first grader, he read ninety books.[2] He also learned to play the piano as a child even though the family could afford only a limited number of lessons.

Neil got his first airplane ride in Warren, Ohio, when he was six years old. A pilot was in town offering local residents rides in his Ford tri-motor airplane. The rates were cheaper on Sunday mornings, and Neil and his dad skipped Sunday school to go. "Neil enjoyed it tremendously," Stephen Armstrong later said, "but I was scared."[3]

When Neil was about halfway through second grade, the family moved to St. Marys, Ohio. Neil enrolled at East Elementary School. Tests showed that he was already reading at a fifth-grade level, and his teacher thought he was too advanced for second grade. She consulted with the school superintendent, and they decided to move him up to the third grade.

Neil made his first model airplane when he was about eight years old, at a cost of ten cents. From

Three-year-old Neil Armstrong was already fascinated with airplanes and flying.

then on, there was always a card table set up somewhere in the house with a model airplane in some stage of development. The rest of the family learned to stay clear of the table. They did not want to disturb any of the scraps of paper or thin strips of balsa wood that Neil used to build his models.

Neil sometimes played football with other boys in the neighborhood, but not for long. He soon wandered back home to read or work on his model airplanes.

As the Armstrong children grew, Stephen Armstrong decided it would be easier for him to commute more so the family would not have to be uprooted as often. As a result, they lived in St. Marys, Ohio, for three years. Then they moved to Upper Sandusky.

Neil was ten years old when he got his first job, mowing grass in a cemetery in Upper Sandusky for ten cents an hour. It was hard work, but his model airplanes were getting bigger, more complicated, and more expensive to build. His parents expected him to earn his own money to pay for the things he wanted.

He later went to work at Neumeister's Bakery, a job he says he probably got because of his size. He was small enough to crawl inside the mixing vats to clean them. He saved the money he earned at the bakery to buy a baritone horn, and then he joined the school band.

Neil was also a Boy Scout, and his father became an assistant scoutmaster in Upper Sandusky. With work, school, and Scouting, Neil's life was sometimes hectic. An example was the day he and a couple of friends from his Boy Scout troop set out on a twenty-mile hike. They were trying to fulfill the requirements they needed to receive a hiking merit badge. By the time they got down to the last three miles, they were all feeling tired. However, Neil was in a hurry to finish because he had to get back in time to work. He ran part of the last three miles. Then he went to work at the bakery until 11:00 P.M.

One of the boys hiking with Neil that day was Konstantine Solakoff, who later became a physician. "I just don't know how he did it," Dr. Solakoff told a reporter, "I was dead tired that evening."[4]

Neil finished elementary school in Upper Sandusky and began his first year of high school there. Then Stephen Armstrong resigned from his job as a state examiner in the auditor's office and began working for the Department of Public Welfare. That spring the family moved to Wapakoneta, Ohio, where Neil's maternal grandparents still lived on their farm outside town. Neil enrolled at Blume High School, which was only about three blocks from his home.

In high school, Neil sang in the glee club, served on the student council, and had a role in the junior class play. He also played the baritone horn in the school band and orchestra, and for a year he was part of a jazz combo called the Mississippi Moonshiners.

The combo was one of the few things Armstrong did purely for enjoyment. John Crites, who taught Neil math, chemistry, and physics, said, "Neil was determined to excel, whether academically or in any other application, and he always had a goal."[5]

His best subjects in high school were math and science. "He was the type of person that people migrated toward," Crites remembered. "The other

A portrait of Neil Armstrong in his school band uniform. He played the baritone horn, an instrument he bought with money he earned by working in a bakery.

students sought him for help and he was such an outstanding student that I let him help me in chemistry and physics lab."[6]

Neil worked at various jobs in Wapakoneta. He was a stock boy for a grocery store, and for a while he worked at a local hardware store. Then he got a job at Rhine and Bradings Pharmacy on Main Street. He went in before school to sweep the floor. After school and on Saturdays, he stocked shelves and waited on customers.

Neil's boss, Richard Brading, described him as a "conscientious, good, hard-working young man,"[7] but he says it was obvious that Neil was not interested in pharmacy. Nor was he interested in the large variety of comic books on display on the store's newsstand. "Neil never bothered reading comic books," Brading said. "Every day he would check the magazine rack to see if any new flying magazines had come in for him to read."[8]

Neil earned forty cents an hour at the pharmacy. He used the money to pay for flying lessons at the local airport, three miles outside town. After work, he hitchhiked out to the airport for lessons that cost nine dollars each. He did not go often because it took him a long time to save up the money for even one lesson.

Neil was interested in flying airplanes, but he also wanted to know how they worked. He learned that by hanging out at the airport where he helped rebuild an old biplane and did odd jobs for the pilots. He also continued to build model airplanes and even constructed a seven-foot wind tunnel in the basement of his family's house where he could test his models. He kept notebooks listing specs and performance records of various aircraft.

Neil was fifteen years old when he got his first close-up look at the moon from the garage of Jacob Zint, Wapakoneta's amateur astronomer. Zint had a homemade observatory on top of his garage with a telescope that could make the moon appear to be within one thousand miles.

Zint said the first time Neil came to his garage was in 1946, when Neil and some of his friends wanted to view a meteor shower. Neil made many return trips. "He would spend a lot of time observing the moon," Zint recalled. "He was always quiet, but after the observing sessions we would speculate on such things as life in space."[9]

On August 5, 1946, Neil celebrated his sixteenth birthday by getting his pilot's license. "I was pretty skinny then—I probably looked twelve or fourteen," Armstrong later said. "I don't suppose anybody would have rented me a secondhand automobile. I didn't have a driver's license, anyway."[10]

His ability to fly was not something Neil boasted about to his friends at school. "I didn't know he had his pilot's license before he was 16," Armstrong's boyhood friend Dudley Schuler once said. "He must have talked about it some, but flying wasn't my interest. Knowing Neil, he probably didn't talk about it much after he realized I wasn't too interested."[11]

At one time, Viola Armstrong thought maybe her son would give up flying after a student pilot he knew was killed in an airplane accident. Neil, his father, and his brother were coming home from Boy Scout camp when they saw the small plane hit a high wire and then crash. Mrs. Armstrong said that her son was very quiet for the next couple of days and he spent a lot of time in his room, but he continued to fly.

Neil dated in high school, but there was no one special girl. "We all dated," Schuler remembers, "but there were no steadies. We went in groups because you could only get the family car once a week. But usually we would just walk a girl home from a school or church activity."[12] Neil liked to joke, but he did it in such a quiet way that sometimes people were not sure he was joking until they saw him smile.

After high school, Neil wanted to go on to college to earn a degree in aeronautical engineering, the study of designing aircraft. He had saved some money for college from his part-time work but not nearly enough. He knew that he would need financial aid. He applied for a United States Navy scholarship and went to Cincinnati to take the two-day qualifying test.

He was later notified by mail that he had been chosen to receive a scholarship. His mother was in the basement getting a jar of fruit when Neil called for her to tell her the news. His shouts startled her, and she dropped the jar on her big toe, turning the toe black and blue. She was not surprised that Neil had gotten a scholarship, but she was surprised that he got so excited about it. Usually, he did not show a lot of emotion.[13]

The scholarship could be used at the school of Neil's choice. He decided to attend Purdue University in West Lafayette, Indiana. His high school teachers recommended the university because it had such a strong aeronautical engineering program.

Because Neil had skipped a grade in elementary school, he was only sixteen years old when he graduated from Blume High School in 1947. That summer he was scheduled to preregister at Purdue University. He thought that trip to West Lafayette would be a good opportunity for a solo flight.

Danger in the Skies

Neil's mother admitted that she was concerned when her sixteen-year-old son wanted to fly solo to West Lafayette, Indiana, to preregister at Purdue University.[1] Her decision to let him go was based, in part, on the fact that Neil rarely made hasty decisions, and he assured her that he had planned carefully for the trip. That morning as he left town, he flew over their house and waggled the plane's wings at his mother, who was out in the yard watching for him.

When classes began that fall, Neil arrived on campus in a more traditional fashion. He and his parents drove the 155 miles to West Lafayette.

Armstrong completed three semesters at Purdue. Then the Navy exercised its option to call him to active duty. He was sent to flight school at Pensacola, Florida, where he trained in single-engine fighters because he said he did not want to be responsible for a crew.[2]

About the time that he was earning his wings, the Korean War (1950–1953) broke out, and Armstrong's skills as a fighter pilot were tested. He was assigned to Fighter Squadron 51, which was based on the West Coast. He was twenty years old and the youngest member of the squadron.

In 1951, the squadron was sent to Korea where Armstrong flew Panther jets off the aircraft carrier *Essex.* He had been trained for air-to-air combat, but since there were no enemy planes in his area, his targets became bridges, trains, and tanks. However, there were times he did come in contact with the enemy.

On September 3, 1951, he was forced to bail out when his plane was hit by enemy fire. "Flak hit the plane, making it unsafe for landing," he later explained. "The plane's control system was knocked out; I could stay in the air, but couldn't land."[3] He flew south out of enemy territory and then parachuted to safety.

A few months later, part of his wing was torn off when he flew his jet down a long narrow valley in North Korea. Communists had stretched a cable across the valley as a booby trap. The cable snagged the wing, tearing it loose, but Armstrong was able to coax his crippled jet back to the aircraft carrier.

Armstrong flew a total of seventy-eight combat missions and earned three air medals, but he downplayed his achievements. "They handed out medals there like gold stars at Sunday School," he said.[4]

Armstrong returned to the United States in the spring of 1952 and received his honorable discharge from the Navy. That fall, he returned to Purdue University. He joined the student chapter of the American Rocket Society, an organization that promoted an interest in rocket and space flight. He was also president of a student flying organization called the Aero Club and a student member of the Institute of Aeronautical Sciences. He played in the Purdue University band and was a member of the Phi Delta Theta fraternity. He also had a job delivering newspapers on campus.

In the early morning hours as he did his newspaper route, he could not help but notice the pretty, dark-haired young woman who was also hurrying across campus. She was Janet (Jan) Shearon, a home economics major from Evanston, Illinois. Shearon's hobby was swimming, and by getting up early to attend 6:00 A.M. labs, she was able to make time for swimming later in the day.

One of the things Armstrong and Shearon had in common was an interest in flying. Shearon's father had been a doctor, and he had owned a small airplane that he used to commute to the family's summer home in Wisconsin. Shearon's mother and her two older sisters had taken flying lessons. However, Jan's father had died when she was twelve years old, before she had a chance to learn to fly.

Shearon and Armstrong became good friends, but they had known each other for a couple of years before he finally asked her out on a date. "Neil is never one to rush into anything," she joked.[5]

Armstrong graduated from Purdue University with a Bachelor of Science (B.S.) degree in aeronautical engineering in January 1955. He applied to the National Advisory Council on Aviation (NACA) to be an aeronautical research pilot at Edwards Air Force Base near Los Angeles, California. There were no openings at Edwards at the time, so Armstrong went to work in NACA's Lewis Flight Propulsion Laboratory in Cleveland, Ohio.

Four months later, he got a call informing him that there was an opening at Edwards Air Force Base. Armstrong says it took him about fifteen seconds to decide to accept the position.

He drove to California, making one detour along the way. That detour was to Wisconsin, where Janet Shearon was working as a camp counselor for the summer. They had already talked about marriage, and Armstrong tried to convince her to marry him immediately and go to California with him. He appealed to her practical side, explaining that he would receive four cents per mile for travel expenses if he made the move himself but six cents per mile if she went with him.

Like Armstrong, Shearon did not like to rush into making decisions. He went to California alone, but not for long. He and Shearon were married a few months later on January 28, 1956. In 1957, their son, Eric (Ricky), was born.

In 1958, the National Aeronautics and Space Administration (NASA) took over NACA's activities.

Neil Armstrong and Janet Shearon were married on January 28, 1956. They met when they were both students at Purdue University.

Armstrong stayed on at Edwards Air Force Base working for NASA as a civilian high-speed test pilot.

That year the Armstrongs moved into a cabin built five thousand feet up in the San Gabriel Mountains. The cabin had no electricity, and although they had cold running water, there was no hot water. Jan Armstrong bathed Ricky in the backyard in a plastic tub. She filled the tub with water and then let the sun warm it to a comfortable temperature for bathing.

The cabin was an hour's drive from Armstrong's work, but the view was spectacular. When Armstrong made test flights, Jan Armstrong could stand in her yard and catch a glimpse of his plane as he streaked over their cabin. With her binoculars, she could see the dust rise when he landed in the valley below.

In his free time, Armstrong worked on modernizing the cabin. He used do-it-yourself books he borrowed from the library as his guides.

Another activity Armstrong enjoyed when he had time off was soaring in a glider. That motorless aircraft is propelled skyward by air currents and pulled back to the ground by the earth's gravity. Armstrong liked the silence and the challenge of gliding. "It's a very demanding sport," he said. "You can't blame the mistakes on anyone but yourself."[6]

In the meantime, the Armstrong family continued to grow. Their daughter, Karen, was born in 1959.

That same year, NASA began seeking the first group of astronauts for its Mercury Project, which was intended to send the first Americans into space in a capsule launched by a rocket.

At that time, Armstrong was not interested in becoming an astronaut.

When Project Mercury came along some of us were a little skeptical. We had wings on our vehicles and the pilot was in complete control—which we thought was a better approach to space flight. So we kind of dismissed the Mercury boys as newcomers to the business.[7]

On November 30, 1960, Armstrong made his first test flight in the X-15 rocket plane that was designed to fly to the edge of the earth's atmosphere. Because the X-15 could haul only a limited amount of fuel, it was carried to a height of forty-five thousand feet under the wing of a B-52 aircraft that had been modified for this purpose. When the B-52 reached that altitude, the X-15 dropped away from it. The X-15 pilot then fired the rocket engine, and the X-15 was propelled toward space.

There was risk involved with every test flight, but one of Armstrong's flights came close to ending in disaster. The X-15 had dropped away from the B-52, and Armstrong went through a series of procedures to fire the X-15's rocket. Nothing happened, and the jet started losing altitude. Armstrong went through each step again. Fortunately, this time it worked. Armstrong never knew why the engine did not fire on the first attempt.

In spite of the danger, Armstrong enjoyed his work. "As a research pilot, I was experiencing the most fascinating time of my life," he said. "I had the opportunity to fly almost every kind of high-performance

Armstrong smiles after completing a test flight in the X-15 research aircraft at the Edwards Air Force Base in California.

airplane and at the same time do research in aerodynamics."[8]

No one was prepared for the news that hit the airwaves on April 12, 1961. On that day, Soviet Yuri Gagarin became the first human in space. He made one orbit around the earth, stunning Americans who had considered themselves more technologically advanced than the Soviets.

However, until then the United States had not made a real commitment to space research. That changed on May 25, 1961, when President John F. Kennedy addressed Congress. He issued a challenge to the American people, saying: "I believe that this nation should commit itself to achieving the goal, before this decade is out, of landing a man on the moon and returning him safely to the earth."[9]

Americans rallied around his challenge. National pride was at stake. They wanted to prove that the United States could be the leader in space. That would not be an easy task. Almost everything about space travel was new, and each small step had to be tested one at a time. Experts estimated that there were more than ten thousand separate tasks that needed to be tested before actually landing a man on the moon.

At that time, in addition to his work on the X-15, Armstrong was involved with the Air Force's Dyna-Soar project. Dyna-Soar was a program to send a winged vehicle into space. Armstrong's work with Dyna-Soar took him to Seattle, Washington.

Since he was going to be there about a month, Jan Armstrong and their two children went with him.

4

Getting on Board

Armstrong was enjoying time with his family in a Seattle park when two-year-old Karen fell as she was running and bumped her head on the ground. She got a nosebleed from the fall and a large goose egg on her head, but she did not appear to be seriously injured.

Then that evening Karen's parents noticed that she was having trouble focusing her eyes. They thought she might have suffered a concussion when her head hit the ground, and the next day they took her to see a Seattle pediatrician. He found no signs of concussion. The family was getting ready to return to California, and the doctor suggested they have Karen examined again when they got home.

In the next couple of weeks while doctors tried to diagnose Karen's problem, she grew progressively worse. She lost her balance and could not walk. Then she could not even crawl. One day her eyes began to roll, and she could not speak plainly. The next day she was admitted to a Los Angeles hospital.

Tests showed that Karen had an inoperable brain tumor. The doctors suspected that the tumor had been there for a while, but there had been no symptoms until her fall.

Armstrong took time off from work, and the whole family went to Los Angeles. There the doctors began radiation treatments using X rays to try to reduce the size of the tumor. The Armstrongs got a room at a nearby motel, and Neil and Jan took turns staying at the hospital with Karen around the clock.

Karen was in the hospital for a week, and then she had another six weeks of treatment as an outpatient. Jan Armstrong stayed in Los Angeles with Karen and Ricky, but Neil Armstrong could not take more time off from work.

At that time, he was working closely with a Minneapolis manufacturer on an adaptive control system he had designed for the X-15. As the X-15 increased in speed, it took less movement to steer it. Pilots had to adjust manually to the change, or they might oversteer and lose control. Armstrong was working on creating a system that adjusted automatically so the pilot could make the same movements at any speed. He was now at a critical stage in its development, only months away from testing it in actual flight.

For the next few weeks, he spent much of his time traveling back and forth between Minneapolis and Los Angeles. He tried to spend as much time as possible with his family and still handle his responsibilities at work.

Gradually, Karen improved. She learned to crawl again and then started to walk. Before long, she was running and playing like a normal two-year-old. The only hint that she had ever been ill at all was a bald spot on her head that had been caused by the X-ray treatments.

Unfortunately, her remission did not last long. About six weeks later, in October, four-year-old Ricky was playing with his sister when he noticed that she was having problems with her eyes again. This time the doctors tried cobalt, which was another radiation treatment. It did not help.

By Christmas, Karen could not walk again, and after the holiday she went steadily downhill. She died shortly before her third birthday on January 28, 1962. It was Neil and Jan Armstrong's sixth wedding anniversary.

A few weeks later, on February 20, astronaut John Glenn orbited the earth three times in the space capsule *Friendship 7*. By that time, Armstrong had begun to reconsider his previous decision not to join NASA's astronaut program. "Dyna-Soar was still earthbound and I began to realize that the Gemini-Apollo programs were going to take man far beyond the mere fringes of the atmosphere and into deep space," he later wrote. "Since this was my real interest, I decided I'd better get aboard."[1]

Astronaut Neil Armstrong. He was one of two civilian astronauts selected in 1962.

On April 18, 1962, NASA announced that it was accepting applications for a second group of astronauts, and Armstrong applied. He was one of 253 qualified applicants screened by NASA in the next few weeks. In June, NASA announced the names of the nine men who had been chosen for the next phase of the space program. Among them were the first two civilian astronauts—Neil Armstrong and Elliott See.

Armstrong made a final test flight in the X-15 on July 26, 1962. Altogether he flew it seven times, reaching a speed of almost four thousand miles per hour and climbing to an altitude of over two hundred thousand feet. That year he also received the Octave Chanute Award from the Institute of Aerospace Sciences. The award was for the work he had done in developing and testing the adaptive control system for the X-15 aircraft.

The next months were busy ones as the family moved to Houston, Texas, and Armstrong began astronaut training. In April 1963, the Armstrongs' second son, Mark, was born.

In addition to the general training that all the astronauts received, each astronaut also specialized in a particular area. Armstrong's specialty was to work on developing simulators.

The simulators looked like the actual space vehicles; however, they never left the ground. Computers were used to make it seem as if the astronauts were in flight. An example was a simulator that duplicated all the sights, sounds, and smells of a launch. A special catastrophe team tried to think of all the malfunctions that could occur during a launch and

Armstrong gets help with his helmet after a test flight in the X-15 research aircraft. Altogether he flew the X-15 seven times, reaching a speed of almost four thousand miles per hour and an altitude of over two hundred thousand feet.

then caused them to happen in the simulator. In that way, the astronauts could learn how to handle various emergencies and how to abort the launch if it became necessary.

In an article for *Life* magazine, Armstrong stressed the importance of using simulators to train astronauts. "For we can't afford to wait until we're in trouble on an actual flight before we start figuring out ways to solve it," he wrote. "We have to think ahead and imagine all of the conceivable emergencies we might face—and then come up with the right conclusions for them without ever leaving the ground."[2]

Armstrong also noted how hard it was to know what type of simulators would be needed because everything about lunar exploration was new. "I do not have an assigned checklist of things to do," he wrote. "I simply have to take a hard look at the missions we have planned and decide for myself which areas we need to work on and how we'll do it."[3]

The Armstrongs had been living in an apartment temporarily while they built a house on a wooded lot in El Lago, Texas, about twenty miles south of Houston near the Manned Spacecraft Center. Neil and Jan Armstrong helped design their new home, which had a swimming pool for Jan and an Asian motif for Neil. During the Korean War, Armstrong had spent some time in Japan, and he had become fond of Japanese art and architecture.

They had been in their new home only a few months when tragedy struck one spring morning in 1964. They awoke about 3:00 A.M. to find their house filled with smoke. Armstrong ran to get their two sons out of the house while Jan Armstrong tried to call the fire department. It was a long-distance call at that time, and Jan Armstrong was too impatient to wait more than a few rings for the operator to answer. She hung up the phone and raced out to the yard to wake up their next-door neighbors, astronaut Edward White and his wife, Pat.

White scaled the six-foot fence that separated their yards and ran to help Armstrong. Armstrong was in the back of the house with Mark, but he could not let go of the toddler. He was afraid his son would fall into the swimming pool in their backyard and drown. White took Mark, and Armstrong went back into the house for Ricky.

By that time, the walls of the house were red from the heat, and the glass in the windows cracked and crumbled to the ground. The cement in back of the house was too hot to stand on, and Jan Armstrong had to keep hosing it down so they could walk across it.

Pat White had been able to get through to the fire department. They could hear the sirens of the fire trucks in the distance as Armstrong came running out of the house with Ricky. He had thrown a wet towel over his son's head to protect him from the fire and smoke.

The cause of the fire was faulty wiring. They had fire insurance, and they rebuilt their home on the same lot. However, they could not put a price tag on the sentimental items that could never be replaced, like the model airplanes that Armstrong had built as a boy. These had been stored in the attic of the house. They did not actually burn in the fire, but they melted and were twisted out of shape. Armstrong kept them anyway, and he later used them as gag gifts for his pilot friends.

Armstrong's training often took him away from home. When he talked with a reporter in October of 1964, he was in the midst of taking geological field trips to explore volcanic ash flows in northern New Mexico and Hawaii. Volcanic ash was believed to be similar to the moon's surface. Armstrong had just presented a paper on astronaut training at an annual meeting for test pilots. Next he was headed to the NASA center at Langley, Virginia, to look into an engineering problem with the lunar module.

It was a hectic schedule, and Armstrong, like the other astronauts, was usually in too much of a hurry to deal with the delays that sometimes occur on commercial airline flights. Instead, he usually flew himself from place to place in a jet fighter trainer, which was supplied by the Air Force for the astronauts' use. It also gave him a chance to keep up his own piloting skills.

Armstrong was assigned to the backup crew for *Gemini 5*. Almost a year later, he became the first civilian in space when *Gemini 8* was launched on March 16, 1966. (The only other civilian astronaut, Elliott See, had been killed when his jet fighter trainer crashed on February 26, 1966, before his first space mission.) The *Gemini 8* flight was to be a three-day mission that would include the first docking in space.

5

"We've Got Serious Problems Here . . ."

President Kennedy's challenge to Americans was not only to land men on the moon but also to return them safely to earth. Docking was a critical part of the return trip. To bring the astronauts back to earth, the lunar landing vehicle would have to be launched from the moon and then rendezvous and dock with a mother ship. So far, docking in space had not been tested. That job fell to Neil Armstrong and David Scott, the *Gemini 8* crew.

As the command pilot for the flight, Armstrong would be the one to guide the *Gemini* spacecraft as it docked with an unmanned Agena satellite, which was to be launched the same day as *Gemini 8*. Armstrong had spent many hours in a simulator practicing this procedure. However, he was also aware of the limitations of simulators.

> *Despite all our training, an actual flight will require a certain amount of old-fashioned "seat-of-the-pants" flying. Bringing two spacecraft together in a rendezvous in space will be like maneuvering a boat into a moving dock in the middle of the night with only a half pint of gas.*[1]

The flight plan also called for astronaut David Scott to do a two-hour extravehicular activity (EVA), more commonly known as a spacewalk. Scott had been one of the fourteen men selected for a third group of astronauts in 1963. He had degrees in science, aeronautics and astronautics, and engineering. He had also been a test pilot.

The launch of *Gemini 8* had been scheduled for March 15, 1966, but it was delayed one day because of mechanical problems with the *Gemini* spacecraft. That night while the astronauts slept, technicians were at work at the launch site, fueling the rockets and making last-minute checks on the equipment. They spotted minor problems in the fuel cell system, the pilots' intercom system, and one of the jet thrusters.

Thrusters were small rockets that the astronauts used to change the position of their spacecraft. Firing a thruster on one side of the vehicle caused the spacecraft to roll. Astronauts then fired a thruster on the opposite side to stop the roll. Thrusters on the rear of the vehicle were fired to fly to a higher altitude, and thrusters on the nose kept it from climbing too high.

In spite of the problems uncovered during the final check of *Gemini 8*, flight preparations were right on schedule when the astronauts were awakened at 7:00 A.M. They climbed into their *Gemini 8* spacecraft only twenty-two minutes before the Agena was scheduled to be launched at 10:00 A.M.

Technicians had set up a television set outside the hatch window so Armstrong and Scott could watch the Agena launch. They saw the Atlas rocket rise off the launchpad. Nine minutes later, the Agena was in orbit 185 miles above the earth.

Armstrong's parents, Stephen and Viola Armstrong, had driven to Florida for the launch. They had just watched the Atlas rocket do its work. Now an even larger Titan rocket waited on the launchpad to carry their oldest son into space aboard the *Gemini 8* spacecraft. They admitted they were nervous. "It is only natural for a father and mother to worry about their children," Stephen Armstrong said, "but to have advance knowledge of their participation in dangerous missions makes it more pronounced."[2]

On the other hand, they were also pleased that their thirty-five-year-old son was finally realizing his dream of flying in space. "I'll be happy for him because I want him to do what he wants and be happy in life," Viola Armstrong said.[3]

Armstrong's brother and sister and their families were also at Cape Kennedy waiting anxiously for the launch. Dean Armstrong, an employee of General Motors, lived in Anderson, Indiana, with his wife and their three children. Armstrong's sister, June, was now Mrs. J. R. Hoffman from Menomonee Falls,

Armstrong waves to reporters as he and David Scott, dressed in their spacesuits, make their way to the Gemini 8 *spacecraft on launch day.*

Wisconsin. She was a nurse, married to a doctor, and they had six children.

Only one part of Armstrong's family was missing—his wife, Jan, and their two sons. They stayed in Houston at Armstrong's request. He wanted to know that his wife was safe at home with their sons while he was in space.

At 11:41 A.M., just as the Agena was completing its first orbit, *Gemini 8* was launched. It arced out over the Atlantic Ocean and disappeared into a clear blue sky. Six minutes and nine seconds into the flight, *Gemini 8* was in orbit ninety-six miles from the earth's surface and twelve hundred miles behind the Agena. In the next four orbits, the astronauts would use some carefully planned maneuvers to catch up to the Agena and prepare for docking.

Since the *Gemini* spacecraft was orbiting at a lower altitude, it had fewer miles to travel than the Agena to complete a revolution. That made it possible for the astronauts to close the twelve-hundred-mile gap between the two vehicles. They used *Gemini*'s thrusters to climb in altitude gradually.

NASA had tracking stations set up on various islands around the world so they could maintain radio contact with the astronauts through each part of their orbit. These were supplemented by two tracking ships, but there were still some "dead zones"—places where the spacecraft was out of contact with any of the tracking stations.

At 4:21 P.M. on *Gemini*'s third orbit, Armstrong reported, "We've got a visual on the Agena at seventy-six miles."[4]

At that time, the Agena was seventy-six miles ahead of the *Gemini* space vehicle. The astronauts could see its beacon light flashing in the black sky. About an hour and fifteen minutes later, Armstrong flew past the Agena and turned the *Gemini* around so that it was now flying backward facing the Agena.

"We're station-keeping . . . ," Armstrong reported. *Gemini* was about 150 feet from the Agena. Both vehicles were traveling at the same rate of speed—17,295 miles per hour.

For the next twenty-five minutes, they flew in this position while Armstrong and Scott checked the Agena's systems electronically to make sure everything was working. Then Armstrong lined *Gemini*'s nose up with the triangular opening of the Agena's docking cone. He fired two of *Gemini*'s rear thrusters, and the space vehicle began edging closer to the Agena at a rate of about three inches per second.

As *Gemini* flew over the tracking ship *Rose Knot Victor* off the coast of Brazil, the Agena's mooring latches clicked. A green indicator light told the astronauts that docking was complete.

"Flight, we are docked!" Armstrong said. "It's a—really a smoothie."

"Roger! Hey, congratulations! This is real good," answered a communicator from the ship.

It was 6:15 P.M.

"Just for your information," Armstrong said, "the Agena was very stable and at the present time we're having no noticeable oscillations at all."

It was good news. There had been some concerns that when the two vehicles connected, the Agena might start to roll. Fortunately, nothing like that had happened.

Over the next thirty minutes, Scott conducted a series of planned tests, including one that told the Agena to fire its thrusters to execute a 180-degree turn, or "yaw."

"It's gone real well," Armstrong reported.

In fact, it appeared that the whole mission was going amazingly well so far. Spirits were high at Mission Control as the day shift prepared to go home and the night shift began to arrive. The astronauts had almost finished their work for the day. Soon, they would be settling down for some well-deserved rest.

The *Coastal Sentry*, a tracking ship off the coast of Formosa (now called Taiwan), picked up the next communication from *Gemini*.

"We have serious problems here," Scott said, "We're—we're tumbling end over end up here. We're disengaged from the Agena."

The problem had begun when the astronauts were in a dead zone and Scott gave the Agena a command to turn on its recorders. Suddenly both vehicles began to roll. Armstrong could counteract the motion by manually firing *Gemini*'s thrusters, so he thought the problem must be with the Agena.

He used *Gemini*'s thrusters to stabilize both vehicles and then he undocked from the Agena. The *Gemini* spacecraft began to roll even faster, spiraling at a rate of one revolution every second. If this continued, the astronauts would become so disoriented that they would no longer be able to see their controls. Soon after that, they would pass out.

Armstrong in a moment of quiet contemplation on board the Gemini 8 spacecraft.

It was at this point that they came into contact with the *Coastal Sentry*. "What seems to be the problem?" the ship's communicator asked.

"We're rolling up and we can't turn anything off," Armstrong answered.

By now, he knew that one of *Gemini*'s thrusters was stuck and firing continuously. However, there were sixteen thrusters. He did not have time to try each one separately, so he shut off all of them.

The *Gemini* continued to spiral. Another thruster would have to be fired in the opposite direction to stop it, and Armstrong had only one choice. There was another set of thrusters—the ones that were to be used to control the spaceship as it reentered earth's gravity. Armstrong used them to bring the spacecraft under control.

"Okay. Relax. Everything's okay," said the communicator from the *Coastal Sentry* after learning that the spiraling was under control.

Unfortunately, everything was not okay. Once the reentry system had been fired, it could develop leaks. There was a chance that *Gemini*'s reentry fuel would leak away in flight and not be available when the astronauts needed it to reenter the earth's atmosphere. NASA had a firm rule for this situation. The astronauts had to return to earth immediately.

At Mission Control, the day crew had stayed on with the night crew, and they all worked together to figure out where to bring the astronauts down. It would be hard, if not impossible, to locate the astronauts if they splashed down in the ocean after dark.

Flight controllers had to find an area where there was still daylight and a rescue team nearby.

Television stations had covered the launch of *Gemini 8* and the docking. Since then, they had gone back to regular programming. Ironically, CBS-TV interrupted a showing of its science fiction series *Lost in Space* to let the audience know that a real space drama was taking place.

Splash Down

Thirty minutes after Mission Control announced that they were bringing the astronauts down, Jan Armstrong drove to the home of Ann Lurton Scott, David Scott's wife. The press was waiting for her in the Scotts' front yard. As she got out of the car, she was blinded by television lights and flashbulbs popping. Reporters shouted questions at her as she hurried past them, but she did not answer.

Armstrong's parents were still in Florida, and they stayed in their motel room watching the reports about the flight on television. NASA arranged to have a hookup with Mission Control placed in their room, and a representative from NASA stayed with them to answer any questions. They were also in contact with Jan Armstrong by telephone.

Flight controllers decided on a splashdown site about five hundred miles southeast of Okinawa, an island in the North Pacific Ocean. The astronauts had one orbit to stow away all their equipment and get ready for reentry. At 9:45 P.M., as they flew over central Africa, Armstrong fired *Gemini*'s reentry rockets.

A half hour later, rescuers aboard a spotter plane saw the spacecraft's giant orange-and-white parachute as it floated toward the ocean. Within minutes, the plane was at the splashdown site, and a three-man rescue team parachuted into the water. They attached a flotation collar to the capsule to keep it afloat and then waited with the astronauts for the rescue ship.

Unfortunately, since it had been an emergency splashdown, there were no rescue ships in the immediate area. The nearest one was the *Leonard F. Mason*, which took three hours to reach them. By that time, the astronauts were violently seasick, and they faced another eighteen hours at sea as the *Mason* made its way to Okinawa.

At first, NASA officials refused to release tapes of the conversations between the astronauts and ground control during the space emergency. Their reluctance caused reporters to speculate that NASA officials were trying to cover up something. There were rumors that the space emergency had been the result of pilot error and that, perhaps, the two astronauts had panicked.

After a day of rest, Armstrong and Scott flew to Cape Kennedy to begin three days of debriefing. Armstrong appeared upbeat when he spoke to a group of about two hundred people who met them at

Armstrong waves to a group of about two hundred people who met the Gemini 8 *astronauts as they arrived at Cape Kennedy. With him is his crewmate, David Scott.*

the landing site in a restricted area at Cape Kennedy. "We had a magnificent flight the first seven hours," he said.[1]

That day NASA released a statement to the press. Robert R. Gilruth, director of the Manned Spacecraft Center, said that their preliminary examination of the information from all the tracking stations had ruled out the possibility of pilot error. "In fact," he said, "the crew demonstrated remarkable piloting skill in overcoming this serious problem and bringing the spacecraft to a safe landing."[2]

Part of the information retrieved from the space capsule included film from a camera that had been mounted in *Gemini 8*'s window. It gave NASA officials a grim look at the wild ride the astronauts had experienced. The camera captured rapid images of light, then darkness as the capsule first faced the sun and then spun away—light, then dark, over and over again until the film ran out.

In NASA's tapes of the conversations between the astronauts and ground control, Armstrong's voice was calm. The only indication of the stress he had felt during the space emergency came from telemetry tapes—electronic signals transmitted from the space capsule to earth. They showed that Armstrong's normal heart rate of seventy-seven beats per minute had almost doubled to one hundred and fifty beats per minute. On March 26, the astronauts were awarded NASA's Exceptional Service Medal for the courage they had shown in the face of an emergency.

Later Armstrong was given a hero's welcome in Wapakoneta, Ohio. At that time, the street where his parents lived was renamed Neil Armstrong Drive. Ohio governor James A. Rhodes also announced that the new airport projected for Auglaize County, where Wapakoneta was located, would be named the Neil Armstrong Airport. Armstrong and his family returned to Wapakoneta in 1967 for the dedication of that airport.

Although the three-day *Gemini* flight ended after a little less than eleven hours, and Scott's EVA had to be scrapped, the mission was considered a success. After all, the most important part of the mission—the first docking in space—had been accomplished.

Four more *Gemini* missions were flown. Armstrong served on the backup crew for *Gemini 11*. Then he was assigned to the Apollo Project—the program that was intended to actually land a man on the moon.

The Apollo Project got off to a tragic start on January 27, 1967, when a fire occurred on board the *Apollo 1* spacecraft while it was still on the launchpad. All three astronauts—Virgil Grissom, Roger Chaffee, and Edward White—died in that fire, which broke out during a launch simulation. The next five Apollo missions were unmanned, and it was almost two years before anyone flew in space again.

However, the astronauts were kept busy with training. After all, most of their work was done on the ground. They spent very little time in space compared to the months of preparation that went into each flight. Armstrong was busy with training and developing flight simulators.

He spent his weekends fishing with his sons and flying gliders with his wife. The whole family enjoyed trips to the ocean for swimming and skin diving.

The Armstrongs did not do a lot of socializing, but they did enjoy having a few friends over for an evening. It was not unusual for their guests to arrive and find Armstrong helping out in the kitchen. Because of his experience working in a bakery when he was young, he had a knack for making dough, and one of his specialties was pizza.

Jan and Neil Armstrong sometimes entertained their friends with a piano duet, but they usually did not get more than a few bars into a song before one or the other of them began to laugh. That would make the other one laugh, and soon the duet was over because they were both laughing too hard to continue.

When they attended large social functions, Jan Armstrong appeared to be at ease laughing and chatting with others. Neil Armstrong, on the other hand, would stand quietly by himself at first. Then, as the evening progressed, he would begin to feel more comfortable, and often he and his wife ended up being the last ones to leave.

In January 1968, the flight crews for *Apollo 8* and *9* were announced. Armstrong was assigned to the backup crew for *Apollo 8*. If NASA continued with its normal rotation schedule, he would be assigned to the *Apollo 11* flight team. At that time, no one knew which mission would be the first lunar landing, but Armstrong, like the other astronauts, was practicing landings in a machine called a lunar landing research vehicle (LLRV).

The astronauts nicknamed the LLRV the "flying bedstead" because it looked so much like a four-poster bed. It was a difficult machine to maneuver. Armstrong probably knew more about how to handle it than anyone else because he had made more flights in it than any other astronaut. One of those flights almost cost him his life.

It was May 6, 1968, and Armstrong was at Ellington Air Force Base in Houston making his twenty-first flight in the LLRV. He took it to a height of five hundred feet, which was standard procedure. Then he began the landing pattern that would be used for a lunar landing. He was down to about two hundred feet when the control system failed, and the vehicle began to spin and lose altitude.

There was a small rocket underneath the pilot's seat that was to be used if the pilot needed to bail out of the LLRV. Until then, no one had ever needed it. Only seconds before the LLRV crashed to the ground and exploded, Armstrong reached down and pulled the D-ring that caused the rocket to fire. The pilot's seat, with Armstrong still sitting on it, shot about two hundred fifty feet into the air. Then Armstrong's parachute opened, and he floated safely to the ground. His only injury was that he bit his tongue.

On January 8, 1909, Deke Slayton, NASA's chief of flight operations, called Armstrong into his office. He told Armstrong that he would be commander of the *Apollo 11* flight, which was scheduled for mid-July or mid-August. By then, the *Apollo 11* mission was targeted as the first lunar landing, but that could change.

The Apollo 11 *crew in their flight suits. From left to right they are: Neil Armstrong, commander; Michael Collins, command module pilot; and Edwin E. Aldrin, Jr., lunar module pilot.*

Everything depended on what was accomplished on other flights before then.

The other astronauts assigned to the *Apollo 11* team were Edwin "Buzz" Aldrin and Michael Collins. Armstrong and Aldrin had worked together on the backup crew for *Apollo 8*. Ironically, it was a medical condition that threatened to end Collins's career that actually got him assigned to the *Apollo 11* crew.

Collins was supposed to fly on the *Apollo 8* mission but was grounded when a loose disk in his neck began pressing on his spinal cord, requiring surgery. The surgery was risky, and doctors were not sure that he would ever be well enough to fly in space again. However, Collins made an amazing recovery, and when doctors cleared him to fly again, he was put on the *Apollo 11* crew.

7

Lift Off!

Armstrong always worked hard, but his training was even more intense during the next few months. His life and the lives of his crewmates depended on how well prepared they were. There was a lot of work to do get ready for the mission, and they had only six months.

Armstrong spent long days in the simulators practicing every detail of the mission. He also prepared for things that could go wrong. Technicians tried to imagine the emergencies that might arise during the mission. Then they programmed their computers to make those emergencies happen in the simulators.

Armstrong practiced lunar landings in a vehicle similar to the one from which he had ejected seconds

Armstrong works in the lunar module simulator in the Flight Crew Training Building at Kennedy Space Center.

before it crashed. That training vehicle had been modified only slightly since his near-fatal accident a year ago.

Armstrong also had to squeeze in time for lunar surface training. He and Aldrin were scheduled to spend two hours and forty minutes on the moon's surface. While they were there, they would gather soil and rock samples, set up scientific experiments, and take photographs. Everything had to be perfectly organized to get it all done during their short stay on the moon.

When Armstrong was not in simulations he was studying the flight manual that detailed every step of the mission. He worked ten- and twelve-hour days, six days a week. Much of his time was spent at the Kennedy Space Center in Florida. When he flew home for a few hours on the weekend, he always took work with him.

Jan Armstrong said the stress of working such long hours was beginning to show. "Neil used to come home with his face drawn white, and I was worried about him," she said. "I was worried about all of them."[1]

Aldrin had another concern. By spring, there had been no announcement from NASA regarding who would take the first step on the moon—Aldrin or Armstrong. Aldrin thought it was something that needed to be decided soon.

Aldrin had assumed that he would be the one. On previous flights, the commander had stayed with the space vehicle while the pilot did the EVA (extravehicular activity). Early reports in the press also indicated that he would be the first one out of the LM.

Then Aldrin began to hear rumors that Armstrong would be the first man out because he was a civilian. "That disturbed me," Aldrin later wrote, "not so much because they'd picked Neil, but because I didn't think it was a very good reason."[2]

Aldrin went to the Apollo program office in Houston and spoke to George Low, who was in charge there. He told Low that he thought a decision should be made soon.

The person to make that decision was Deke Slayton, NASA's chief of flight operations. About a week later, Slayton told the astronauts that Armstrong would be the first man out of the LM. He gave two reasons for his decision. For one thing, Armstrong had more seniority in the astronaut program. The other reason was a practical one. Because Aldrin was the LM pilot, he would stand on the right side of the LM during the descent to the moon. Considering the location of the hatch and the direction it opened, it would be easier for Armstrong to be the first one out and the last one in.

Aldrin said he was satisfied with the explanation, but Michael Collins thought he noticed a change in Aldrin after that. "Buzz's attitude took a noticeable turn in the direction of gloom and introspection shortly thereafter," Collins later wrote.[3]

Armstrong kept his thoughts to himself as he usually did. Although the three astronauts spent long hours together preparing for the *Apollo 11* mission, they rarely discussed personal feelings. The lack of communication between the astronauts amazed Collins, who later wrote that Armstrong "never transmits anything but the surface layer, and that very sparingly. I like him, but I don't know what to make of him, or how to get to know him better."[4]

Reporters were also learning that it was difficult to get to know Neil Armstrong. The *Apollo 11* mission, more than any other flight, had captured public and media attention. It had been eight years since President Kennedy had issued the challenge to land a man on the moon before the decade was out. *Apollo 11* was the mission that might meet that goal.

Armstrong was becoming a new American hero. He appeared to have the right qualities for that role. He was hardworking, courageous, and cool-headed. On the other hand, he looked as if he could have been the boy next door. His blond hair, blue eyes, and a slightly lopsided grin made him look boyish even though he was thirty-eight years old. Americans wanted to know all about him.

However, publicity was not something Armstrong welcomed. He seemed hesitant to talk to reporters. He answered their questions slowly, taking time to think about what he wanted to say before he began to speak. He avoided talking about his personal life, and he did not show much emotion.

This brought mixed reactions from members of the press. Some said he was quiet, shy. Others found him to be cold or downright difficult. After an interview with Armstrong, one reporter wrote: "He talked reluctantly, grudgingly, almost contemptuously. He disdains all talk about people. He prefers to talk about ideas and hardware . . ."[5]

At a press conference in 1989, Armstrong shared his memories of the first lunar landing. From the start, astronaut Neil Armstrong valued his privacy and did not talk to reporters about his personal life.

Reporters who tried to find out how Armstrong felt were often disappointed. A typical Armstrong answer was the one he gave when a reporter asked him how he felt about being the first man on the moon:

> *I'm certainly not going to say I'm without emotion at the thought, because that wouldn't be factual. But I think more about day-to-day things that have to be done—the factual parts of touching down on the lunar surface and doing this and that job. I don't think very much about the emotional aspects . . .*[6]

Armstrong was often asked if he thought about the dangers of the mission.

> *I don't have any fears for myself. But I am concerned about how problems would affect the space program and the country's reaction. It is silly to say we don't think of the dangers. We do all the time. But our job is to make those dangers less and less. I don't think of it as a personal danger.*[7]

In a lighter moment, he half-jokingly said, "What I really want to be, in all honesty, is the first man back from the moon."[8]

Jan Armstrong also thought about the danger. She found the best way for her to deal with her fears was to learn as much as she could about the mission. She said Neil was a patient teacher, taking time to explain the technical parts of the flight to her.

Armstrong was equally patient in answering his sons' questions. By the time of the *Apollo 11* mission, twelve-year-old Ricky knew a lot about space travel and even six-year-old Mark understood what was going to happen. "My daddy's going to the moon," he told a reporter. "It will take him three days to get there. I want to go to the moon someday with my daddy."[9]

However, most of the time Ricky and Mark were more concerned with their normal childhood activities. Ricky was playing on a baseball team, and Mark was the team's bat boy.

On May 18, 1969, *Apollo 10* was launched from Cape Kennedy with astronauts Thomas Stafford, John Young, and Eugene Cernan. On that mission, while Young orbited the moon in the CM, Stafford and Cernan climbed into the LM and undocked from the CM. They orbited the moon in the LM, coming within ten miles of the moon's surface. Then they docked with the CM and returned home, splashing down on May 26.

The success of that mission meant that, so far, every step for a lunar landing had been tested except for the actual landing on the moon's surface. It was now certain that the *Apollo 11* astronauts would make that first attempt.

In June, the three astronauts moved into crew quarters on Merritt Island near the Kennedy Space Center. "We needed a month sealed off from the world, to live and relive the complex venture before us," Collins later wrote, "and crew quarters was the only place to do that."[10]

Armstrong did fly home to spend the Fourth of July weekend with his family. It was his last trip home before the mission. After that, the astronauts were semiquarantined to protect them from being exposed to any illnesses that might delay their flight.

They had contact with their families and the people they worked with at NASA, but no one else.

NASA's determination to protect the astronauts from germs accounted for the elaborate setup for the last press conference the astronauts held before their flight. On July 14, in a thirty-minute nationally televised news conference, the astronauts were questioned by four reporters. The reporters had been handpicked by NASA from more than three thousand members of the press who were in Florida to cover the launch. They were not allowed in the same room as the astronauts, so they interviewed them by closed-circuit television from a room fifteen miles away.

Although Armstrong did not like his family to travel when he was in space, Jan Armstrong did not want to miss the *Apollo 11* launch. She planned to watch the launch from a friend's boat on the Banana River about four miles from Cape Kennedy. Ricky and Mark traveled to Florida with her.

About midnight the night before the launch, Jan Armstrong drove out to Cape Kennedy. She wanted one last look at the spacecraft that would carry her husband a quarter of a million miles into space. There, on launchpad 39A, the Saturn V rocket towered 363 feet into the air. On top of it sat the space capsule, looking very small in comparison to the rocket. At night, the rocket was illuminated by floodlights, and a spotlight highlighted the American flag on its side. It was an unforgettable sight.

Launch day began at 4:15 A.M. when Deke Slayton, the director of flight operations, knocked on Armstrong's door. Armstrong showered and then had

Neil Armstrong with his family about the time of the Apollo 11
*flight. Jan Armstrong holds Mark, and in back is their older son,
Eric, who was nicknamed Ricky.*

one final checkup in a small examination room that had been set up near the astronauts' rooms. He joked with nurse Dee O'Hara, and when the exam was over, he winked at her and smiled. He did not say good-bye. The astronauts never said good-bye on launch day.

At 5:00 A.M., the astronauts had a breakfast of steak and eggs, a meal Armstrong would have liked to skip. Normally he did not eat breakfast at all, especially when he was busy training. Then it was a cup of coffee as he was heading out the door, and often he did not take time for lunch either.

After breakfast, the astronauts put on their bulky white space suits and then climbed into a white NASA van for the five-mile drive to the launch site. They took a special route to avoid the traffic jams caused by people who had come to watch the launch.

More than a million spectators were in the area. Every motel room within a fifty-mile radius was filled. Those who could not get motel rooms camped in their cars or pitched tents on the beach.

There were another six thousand people who were invited guests of NASA. These included United States congressmen, ambassadors, and governors from several states. Armstrong's brother, Dean, and his sister, June Hoffman, were among those guests who sat in a special grandstand that NASA had built about a mile from the launch site.

The Hoffmans had added another family member since the *Gemini 8* launch, making a total of seven children. June Hoffman, her husband, and their older children would watch the launch from the grandstand. The younger children stayed with Dr. Hoffman's

Apollo 11 *was launched at 9:32* A.M. *on July 16, 1969. An estimated 528 million people watched live coverage of the launch on television.*

parents, who lived in Florida. Dean Armstrong was joined by his wife and their oldest son, Jay.

Armstrong's parents decided they would be more comfortable at home in Wapakoneta during the mission. Several days before the launch, a NASA official moved in with them as a combination security person and reference person for any questions they might have during the flight.

Armstrong was the first one to enter the *Apollo* spacecraft at 6:52 A.M. He took the left couch next to the abort handle. As flight commander, he would be the one to abort the mission if necessary. Collins was on the right couch and Aldrin in the middle.

A loudspeaker at the Cape kept the people who had come to watch the launch informed about the progress.

"Thirty seconds and counting. Astronauts report it feels good. T minus twenty-five seconds. Twenty seconds and counting. T minus fifteen seconds. Guidance is internal. Twelve, eleven, ten, nine, ignition sequence starts . . ."[11]

The five engines of the Saturn V rocket began to rumble. Steam rose up around the rocket as water sprayed onto the launchpad to keep it cool.

". . . six, five, four, three, two, one, zero, all engines running."[12]

The ground shook and there was a deafening roar as the rocket began to rise.

"Lift off! We have a lift off! Thirty-two minutes past the hour. Lift off on *Apollo 11*."[13]

8

"The *Eagle* Has Landed"

Two and a half minutes into the flight, the first stage of the Saturn V rocket shut down and fell back into the Atlantic Ocean. Four seconds later, the second stage fired and burned for about six minutes. Then it, too, separated from the spacecraft, and a third engine fired, sending the spacecraft into orbit around the earth.

The astronauts made one and a half orbits around the earth. Then they got a go ahead from the Manned Spacecraft Center for the next part of the flight.

"*Apollo 11*, this is Houston. You are GO for TLI."[1]

The initials "TLI" stood for translunar injection. The third stage of the rocket fired again, sending the spacecraft out of orbit and on its way to the moon.

"Hey, Houston, *Apollo 11*. That Saturn gave us a magnificent ride," Armstrong radioed back to Mission Control.[2]

The astronauts had begun their three-day trip to the moon. For the next two days, they were busy with routine tasks. They cleaned and checked equipment. They also had regular televised broadcasts to earth.

In El Lago, Jan Armstrong watched eagerly for those glimpses of her husband on her television screen. After the launch at Cape Kennedy, she and the couple's two sons had flown back to Houston on a private jet. She spent much of the first days of the flight in the master bedroom of their home. She was surrounded by maps and charts to help her follow the *Apollo 11* flight as closely as possible.

Nearby was the squawk box—a small speaker, about four inches by four inches. It was connected to Mission Control by telephone line. Through it the wives could listen to communications between the astronauts and Mission Control.

By the weekend, relatives had arrived at the Armstrong home. They planned to be with Jan Armstrong when the lunar landing took place. Her mother, Louise Shearon, came in from Pasadena, California. Her sister Nancy, her husband, and their two teenage children came from Pennsylvania. Jan's other sister, Carolyn, and her husband and children arrived from Chicago. Neil's brother, Dean, and his wife and son flew in from Cape Kennedy. They had stayed in Florida to rest for a couple of days before making the trip to Houston.

Jan Armstrong talks to reporters in front of the Armstrong home in El Lago, Texas. With her are the Armstrongs' two sons, twelve-year-old Ricky and six-year-old Mark.

Other astronauts arrived at the Armstrong home during critical periods of the flight. They were there to answer any questions Jan Armstrong had about the mission. Astronaut John Young was there on Saturday when it was time for *Apollo 11* to begin an engine burn. This procedure would slow down the spaceship and allow it to be captured by the moon's gravity. If the burn did not work, they would circle the moon and then boomerang back toward earth. No one on earth would know the result of the burn for a while because *Columbia,* the command module, had flown behind the moon. The astronauts were out of contact with Mission Control.

Collins gave the report on the burn when they reestablished radio contact with ground control. "It was like—it was like perfect," he said.[3] *Apollo 11* was orbiting the moon.

That night the astronauts got only five or six hours of sleep. They were up early the next morning to prepare for the lunar landing. After breakfast, Aldrin put on his pressurized space suit and crawled through the tunnel to the LM to begin a series of checks. Armstrong joined him about an hour later.

At 1:46 P.M., *Columbia* orbited behind the moon, and the lunar module, *Eagle,* undocked from the command module. Armstrong and Aldrin began their descent to the moon's surface.

"There were some scary things during that descent," Armstrong recalled. "Especially those computer alarms."[4]

Millions of people all over the world heard Armstrong's words when the LM finally touched down. "Houston, Tranquility Base here. THE *EAGLE* HAS LANDED."[5]

It was 4:18 P.M. in New York City, where a baseball game at Yankee Stadium was interrupted to announce that the astronauts had landed on the moon. Sixteen thousand fans stood up and sang "The Star-Spangled Banner."

Armstrong and Aldrin spent the next three hours after their landing checking out all of the *Eagle*'s systems. They had to make sure that the LM was ready to go if they had to leave the moon in a hurry. The flight plan then called for a four-hour rest period, but the astronauts were too excited to rest. They asked Mission Control for permission to begin their EVA earlier than planned, and Houston agreed.

The astronauts ate their first meal on the moon inside the LM. Then they began to get ready to walk on the moon. Their space suits included a backpack, which was their portable life-support system (PLSS). With the PLSS, each astronaut would become his own miniature spacecraft with his own oxygen supply, temperature control, and communications equipment. It was their only protection in a hostile environment. Temperatures on the moon range from 121°C (250°F) above zero to more than 121°C (250°F) below zero. There is no air or water.

When they were suited up, they had to depressur ize the LM cabin before they could open the hatch. The whole process of getting ready took longer than anyone expected. At the Armstrong home, everyone crowded around the television set in the living room and waited. They wondered why it was taking

Armstrong so long to come out. Jan Armstrong joked that it was because he was trying to decide what he was going to say. For weeks, people had been asking Armstrong what his first words would be. However, he had been so busy with training that he had not had time to think about it. Now, millions of people around the world would hear those first words together.

As Armstrong started down the ladder, he stopped to pull a handle that lowered a camera mounted on the outside of the LM. It enabled people on earth to watch on their television screens as Armstrong's shadowy figure backed down the ladder.

Then he stepped off the bottom rung and onto the moon's surface. "That's one small step for a man, one giant leap for mankind," he said.[6]

Unfortunately, his words were garbled in the transmission and people thought he said, "one small step for man."[7] It was a minor variation, but Armstrong was particular in choosing his words. He said he could only speak for himself, but when the "a" was omitted, it made it sound as if he were speaking for all mankind.

"And the surface is fine and powdery," Armstrong said as he began to walk on the moon. "I can—I can pick it up loosely with my toe. It does adhere in fine layers like powdered charcoal to the sole and sides of my boots. I only go in a small fraction of an inch, maybe an eighth of an inch, but I can see the foot-prints of my boots and the treads in the fine, sandy particles."[8]

His words put an end to fears some scientists had expressed. They thought that perhaps the moon was

Armstrong's footprint on the moon. "That's one small step for a man, one giant leap for mankind," he said as he stepped onto the moon's surface.

not solid and that the astronauts would sink into the soil when they tried to walk across it.

There had been others who thought the astronauts might not be able to walk in the bulky space suits with their heavy backpacks. They thought the astronauts might just topple over. Armstrong answered their questions, too.

"There seems to be no difficulty in moving around as we suspected. It's even perhaps easier than the simulations at one-sixth g that we performed . . . on the ground. It's actually no trouble to walk around."[9]

Armstrong's first priority was to scoop up about two pounds of lunar soil, bag it, and stow it away in a special pocket on the thigh of his space suit. These were the contingency samples. If the astronauts had to leave the moon in a hurry, they would not go home empty-handed.

Then he began to describe his surroundings.

"It has a stark beauty all its own," he said. "It's like much of the high desert of the United States. It's different but it's very pretty out here."[10]

"Beautiful view!" Aldrin commented as he joined Armstrong on the surface.[11]

"Isn't that something!" Armstrong replied. "Magnificent sight out here."[12]

Armstrong removed the camera from the LM and set it up on a tripod about thirty feet away. The astronauts wandered in and out of the view of the camera as they did their work on the moon.

A plaque was mounted on the bottom half of the LM, the part that would remain on the moon. Armstrong read the inscription on the plaque to the television

Armstrong took this photograph of Aldrin in front of the lunar module while the astronauts were on the moon's surface.

audience on earth. "Here men from the planet Earth first set foot upon the Moon, July 1969 A.D. We came in peace for all mankind."[13] The plaque also had the signatures of the three astronauts of *Apollo 11* and the signature of President Nixon.

Armstrong and Aldrin also planted an American flag on the moon's surface. Since there is no wind on the moon, the flag was stiffened with a thin piece of wire to make it look as if it were flying.

There were also other small items that the astronauts would leave on the moon. One of these was a one-and-a-half-inch silicone disk that contained goodwill messages from around the world. There were messages from the former presidents Eisenhower, Kennedy, and Johnson; a message from President Nixon; and messages from the leaders of seventy-two other countries. They also left a patch from *Apollo 1* in memory of the three astronauts who had died in the fire on the launchpad and the medals of two Soviet cosmonauts who had died—Yuri Gagarin and Vladimer Komarov.

After they had been on the moon about fifty minutes, Mission Control asked the astronauts to move in front of the camera to receive a telephone call from President Nixon. The President said:

> *For one priceless moment in the whole history of man, all the people on this Earth are truly one; one in their pride in what you have done and one in our prayers that you will return safely to Earth.*[14]

"Thank you, Mr. President," Armstrong replied. "It's a great honor and privilege for us to be here representing not only the United States, but men of peace of all nations . . ."[15]

Along with gathering soil and rock samples, Armstrong and Aldrin had three scientific experiments to set up. One of the experiments was a laser reflector that would help scientists measure the distance between the moon and earth more accurately. They also set up a seismic detector that would measure shock vibrations on the moon, or "moonquakes." The third experiment was a solar-wind detector to help scientists determine if any lunar gases existed on the moon's surface.

Aldrin took this picture of Armstrong inside the lunar module after the astronauts had finished their work on the moon's surface.

About two and a half hours after Armstrong's first step on the moon, the astronauts climbed back inside the LM. They took off their space suits. Then they reopened the hatch to toss out any equipment they did not need for the return flight. It was an attempt to make the LM as lightweight as possible for lift off from the moon. Their discards included space suits, backpacks, boots, cameras, and tools used to collect soil samples.

The seismic detector that the astronauts had set up on the moon was very sensitive. Mission Control recorded vibrations for each piece of equipment the astronauts dropped.

"We observed your equipment jettison on the TV, and the passive seismic experiment recorded shocks when each PLSS hit the surface," the capcom remarked.[16]

"You can't get away with anything anymore, can you?" Armstrong joked.[17]

The astronauts ate and then tried to get some rest. Their day had begun on the *Columbia* at 5:30 A.M. It was now after midnight. However, they still found it hard to sleep. It was cold inside the LM, and there was no room to lie down.

After a restless sleep period, the astronauts were ready to blast off and reunite with *Columbia*—twenty-one hours after landing on the moon. The lunar module's ascent engine had been tested more than three thousand times before the *Apollo 11* mission, but that did not mean anything if it did not work now. Armstrong reached out to pull the switch to fire the rocket but discovered it had been broken off.

Apparently, it had been snagged by one of their space suits.

There were tense moments as the astronauts searched for a way to replace the broken switch. Their lifesaver was a felt-tipped pen that fit perfectly into the slit. The engine fired, and the top half of the LM lifted easily off the moon's surface. Within four hours, the *Eagle* had rendezvoused and docked with the CM.

Armstrong and Aldrin transferred the soil samples and other equipment to the CM. Then Michael Collins pulled a switch, and the *Eagle* was jettisoned into space. The LM would orbit the moon for a while and then eventually crash on the moon's surface.

On their last orbit around the moon, Michael Collins fired *Columbia*'s engines again. The CM gained speed and broke out of the moon's gravity.

From Mission Control, capcom Charlie Duke wanted a report on the burn. "How did it go?" he asked.[18]

"Tell them to open up the LRL doors, Charlie," Armstrong answered.[19] The LRL was the lunar receiving laboratory where the astronauts would be quarantined when they returned to earth.

"Roger," Duke said. "We got you coming home."[20]

After the Moon

Two and a half days later, on July 24, the astronauts splashed down in the Pacific Ocean. Before the *Apollo 11* mission, NASA officials had tried to protect the astronauts from contagious illnesses that might delay their flight. Now it was the other way around; they were concerned with protecting everyone else from moon germs.

Scientists were reasonably certain that there was no life on the moon. On the other hand, they could not take even the slightest risk that the astronauts might bring back unknown germs that could start a mysterious epidemic on earth. As a safeguard, the astronauts were to be quarantined for three weeks. The moon rocks were quarantined for sixty days.

NASA also took precautions to make sure that those aboard the rescue ship U.S.S. *Hornet* did not come into direct contact with the astronauts. Frogmen wearing special biological isolation garments (BIGs) opened the hatch of the *Apollo 11* spaceship and tossed BIGs inside for each of the astronauts. The astronauts wore the garments while they were being transferred from the capsule to a special isolation van on the *Hornet*.

President Nixon was on deck to welcome the astronauts home, but he expressed his greetings through a window in the isolation van. "This is the greatest week in the history of the world since the Creation," he said.[1]

A NASA physician on the *Hornet* gave the astronauts preliminary medical exams. He found they were all healthy except for Armstrong, who had a slight ear infection. The doctor said the infection was probably caused by a buildup of pressure inside the ear during reentry into the earth's atmosphere.

Sixty-seven hours after the astronauts splashed down in the Pacific Ocean, the *Hornet* docked at Pearl Harbor. The astronauts, still inside the isolation van, were taken by helicopter to Hickman Air Force Base. They were loaded onto an Air Force C-141 transport jet and flown to Houston. There the van was rolled onto a flatbed truck and taken to the specially designed lunar receiving laboratory (LRL) at the Manned Spacecraft Center.

During the quarantine, the LRL would be home to the astronauts and twelve other people. These included three doctors (one for each astronaut), technicians,

Armstrong looks up from a newspaper to listen to a conversation between Michael Collins, left, and Edwin Aldrin, Jr. They are inside a special isolation van on their way to the lunar receiving laboratory at the Manned Spacecraft Center.

a cook, and a public relations person. Each of the astronauts had his own small bedroom. There was also a kitchen, a dining area, a lounge, and an exercise room. The astronauts could watch television, play cards, shoot pool, or enjoy a game of table tennis. However, they did not have much time for any of those things. Much of their time was spent in debriefings—that is, discussions with NASA officials about the flight. There were also medical tests.

Armstrong celebrated his thirty-ninth birthday in the LRL on August 5. He could see his family through a large window, and they could talk to each other using a speaker system. It would be another five days before they could celebrate together in person.

The astronauts showed no signs of contamination from moon germs, and when the quarantine ended, the world was ready to welcome them home. On August 13, the men and their wives embarked on a whirlwind one-day tour through three cities across the United States. It began with a ticker-tape parade in New York City. Then the astronauts hopped on a jet and flew to Chicago for another parade.

The day ended in Los Angeles with a state dinner hosted by President and Mrs. Nixon at the Century Plaza Hotel. There were over fourteen hundred guests, including congressmen, governors, the President's cabinet, and foreign dignitaries. Armstrong's parents were also invited. Viola Armstrong was faced with an unusual dilemma when she saw the President of the United States and her son approaching her at the same time. It was the first time she had seen her son since the quarantine.

"They were both coming towards me," she remembered. "I thought I should shake the president's hand, but then I saw Neil. I said, 'Excuse me, Mr. President, I have to get my son.'"[2]

At that dinner, the President awarded the astronauts the Presidential Medal of Freedom, the highest United States civilian award.

That one-day tour was only the beginning of the parades and celebrations that were to come. On September 6, Armstrong and his family traveled to Wapakoneta, Ohio, for another full day of activities.

The day began at 9:30 A.M. when Armstrong addressed hundreds of students on the high school football field. At Armstrong's request, only those who were seventeen and younger were allowed to attend. That was followed by a short reunion with his 1947 high school graduation class. Then there was a forty-minute press conference and appearances at two luncheon banquets. All of these activities took place before the parade, which was scheduled for 1:20 P.M.

Comedian Bob Hope was grand marshal for the parade, which featured twenty-three bands, including the Purdue University marching band. Later in the day, Hope served as emcee for a homecoming program held at the fairgrounds. After the day's events, Armstrong and his family flew back to Houston.

NASA had also organized a world tour for the astronauts and their wives. They traveled to twenty-seven cities in twenty-four countries in forty-five days.

When the tour ended, Armstrong accepted a desk job at NASA headquarters in Washington, D.C. His official title was deputy associate administrator for aeronautics. His job was to coordinate and manage NASA's aeronautical research and technology. He also completed work for a master of science (M.S.) degree in aerospace engineering, which he received from the University of Southern California in 1970.

Armstrong was trying to live the private life of an ordinary citizen, but that was not easy to do. Being the first man on the moon had brought him fame that he did not appreciate.

He was contacted by motion-picture producers and publishers who wanted to tell his story. There

Astronauts Michael Collins, Neil Armstrong, and Edwin Aldrin, Jr., wave to the thousands of people who lined the streets to welcome them in Sydney, Australia. This was just one stop in their forty-five-day world tour.

were offers for lucrative contracts from companies who wanted Armstrong to endorse their products and lecture agents who wanted to represent him. In Wapakoneta, a Neil Armstrong museum was under construction, and local merchants were selling Neil Armstrong T-shirts and other souvenirs.

Armstrong was also a subject for gossip colum nists who linked him romantically with various Hollywood actresses. He received thousands of letters, including love letters from women he had never met. There was also hate mail containing serious threats.

Just as disappointing for Armstrong was the fact

that Americans appeared to be losing interest in space exploration. Armstrong considered the *Apollo 11* mission to be a beginning. "The manned probe of the moon is a vital and thrilling experiment," he once said, "but there are many more fascinating experiments in the future."[3]

However, for many Americans, landing a man on the moon had been the goal. Once it was reached, they turned their attention to problems closer to home, such as poverty and the war in Vietnam. Altogether there have been six lunar landings, but none of them captured the public's attention like the first.

In 1971, Armstrong resigned from NASA and accepted a position as professor of aerospace engineering at the University of Cincinnati. In addition to teaching, Armstrong was also involved in research at the university, primarily focusing on ways to apply space technology to earth uses.

One of his projects was an improved pump for the heart-lung machines used in open-heart surgery. That pump was an adaptation of one NASA had developed to circulate fluid in the astronauts' space suits. One of the members of Armstrong's research team was Dr. Henry Heimlich, who developed the Heimlich maneuver for choking.

Armstrong commuted to the university from a farm he bought in Lebanon, Ohio, about thirty miles from Cincinnati. His sons attended school in Lebanon, and Jan Armstrong helped on the farm and did volunteer work for the schools. On Friday nights during the summer, Neil and Jan Armstrong played

Armstrong teaches a class in aerospace engineering at the University of Cincinnati.

golf with a group of friends. "I have chosen to bring my family up in as normal an environment as possible," Armstrong explained.[4]

He had guarded his privacy as an astronaut. As a private citizen, Armstrong appears even more determined to avoid the limelight. He lives quietly in Lebanon. People see him around town, but few of them actually talk to him. "To most of his neighbors, Armstrong may as well be the man on the moon," a reporter once wrote.[5]

Armstrong developed a policy of speaking to the press only through news conferences, which he holds about once a year. He decided he would not give individual interviews.

> *I have never backed off from honest inquiries. The only thing I've done is say, "Gee, I'm not going to spend all day every day with every guy who's trying to put a book together, put a magazine article together or put a newspaper feature together."*[6]

A writer for *Life* magazine observed that Armstrong "is capable of cold, tight-lipped rage."[7] That part of his personality surfaces most often when he feels people are trying to exploit him or use his status as the first man on the moon to promote their own interests. An example was an Earth Day celebration held at the University of Cincinnati. Armstrong had been invited to participate, and he had agreed. However, he was disturbed when he found out that the university was advertising that their "spaceman" would be there.[8]

According to a Cincinnati newspaper, Armstrong called the public relations director at the university and asked, "How long must it take before I cease to be known as a spaceman?"[9]

On the other hand, Armstrong has participated in some community projects. He was chairman of Cincinnati's 1973 Easter Seal Drive. In 1976, he helped raise money for a $6.5 million YMCA in Lebanon and was one of the original board members. He has also been a member of the Warren County Airport Board.

He has also accepted some public speaking engagements. He hired a lecture agent to handle the hundreds of requests he received each year. The few offers he has accepted were for groups or causes that were important to him.

Because he had been a Boy Scout for many years, he has made several appearances on their behalf. He has also made appearances in support of conservation and protecting the environment, an interest that is a direct result of the *Apollo 11* mission. A thought that occurred to Armstrong when he was in space looking down on earth was that it was a fragile planet and needed to be protected.

Armstrong usually turns down offers to endorse products. However, he did appear in advertisements for quartz crystal watches for the General Time Corporation, and he has served as a spokesperson for the Chrysler Corporation. He also did a television commercial for Bankers Association of America. "I've worked in some commercial arrangements off and on, on kind of a modest basis," he said. "I've taken the position that, if the right situation came along, where I thought I could be of significant help . . . and it would not jeopardize my honesty . . ."[10]

It appears that the privacy Armstrong desires has a lot to do with choice. He can choose which appearances he wants to make and the causes he wants to support. When he desires privacy, he can retreat to his farm, where he grows corn and raises cattle.

In October 1978, Armstrong became one of the first group of six astronauts to receive the Congressional Space Medal of Honor. That award is presented to astronauts who have done something exceptional in space.

Ironically, after being involved in high-risk occupations much of his life as a fighter pilot, test pilot, and an astronaut, Armstrong's most serious injury came in an accident on his farm in November 1978. He was jumping down from a truck when his wedding ring caught on a barn door and tore off his ring finger. He was taken to a hospital in Cincinnati and then transferred to a hospital in Louisville, Kentucky. The surgeons successfully reattached the finger.

In 1979, Armstrong cut back to a part-time teaching position at the University of Cincinnati. He said he wanted to devote more time to his farm and to testing jets for the Gates Learjet Corporation. In February 1979, he set an altitude record for business jets at fifty-one thousand feet.

By the end of the year, he resigned altogether from the university. He accepted a position as chairman of the board for the Cardwell International Corporation in Lebanon, Ohio.

In 1982, he became chairman of Computing Technologies for Aviation, Inc. (CTA). The company supplies computer information management systems for business aircraft. Since then, he has served on the boards of many corporations, such as Gates Learjet, Cincinnati Gas & Electric, Taft Broadcasting, and Marathon Oil.

In 1984, Armstrong accepted an appointment to the National Commission on Space (NCOS), a presidential panel appointed to plan a national space program to take the country into the twenty-first century. However, before the panel completed its report, the space shuttle *Challenger* exploded seconds after launch on January 28, 1986. Armstrong was named vice chairman of the Rogers Commission, a committee formed to investigate that accident. The results of that investigation were that a faulty O-ring seal on one of the solid rocket boosters had caused the accident.

Although Armstrong has remained active, he has managed to stay out of the public eye. His success in living a private life became especially evident in 1994. In April of that year, he and his wife were divorced after thirty-eight years of marriage. The news did not make headlines and, in fact, was barely mentioned until a couple of months later when the country began to celebrate the twenty-fifth anniversary of the lunar landing.

The Man Beyond the Moon

In July 1994, people all across the country were celebrating the twenty-fifth anniversary of the first lunar landing. Collins and Aldrin returned to Cape Canaveral (formerly Cape Kennedy) for anniversary ceremonies, but Armstrong did not join them.

The people of Wapakoneta threw a weeklong party, but Armstrong did not appear. It made some people in the community angry. "Your hometown puts on a big festival celebrating the 25-year anniversary of something you did, the least you could do is show up," one man said.[1]

Reporters from all over the world flocked into Lebanon hoping to get a story about Armstrong. Tom

Armstrong participated in a press conference at NASA headquarters in June 1989 commemorating the twentieth anniversary of the Apollo 11 *mission.*

Barr, the local newspaper editor, was kept busy shuttling reporters out to Armstrong's home, showing them where he lived.

There were reports that Armstrong had already remarried. It was a surprising development from a man who typically did not rush into anything. Reporters were determined to get information about Armstrong's divorce and remarriage. However, as far as Barr knows, none of them were successful.

The court records for Armstrong's divorce were sealed, which meant that information about those proceedings was not open to the public. Armstrong was not available for comment.

A reporter for *The New York Times* described how difficult it was to get information about Armstrong from the people in Lebanon. "Outsiders inquiring about Mr. Armstrong were summarily turned away by the otherwise pleasant clerks at the public library," he wrote. "The woman in charge at the local airstrip where he keeps an airplane was no help either. And at the Village Ice Cream Parlor a waitress said, 'He's quiet and doesn't like publicity, and no one will say anything about him.'"[2]

Information about Jan Armstrong and the couple's grown sons was also unavailable.

Armstrong did make one unscheduled appearance in honor of the twenty-fifth anniversary of the lunar landing. He showed up at an airshow at the Neil Armstrong Airport in New Knoxville, Ohio, on July 17, 1994. He signed autographs and spoke with reporters, but when a biplane flew overhead, he looked up at it and said, "I wish I was up there."[3]

At the Neil Armstrong Museum in Wapakoneta, Ohio, busloads of children file in to see the *Gemini 8* space capsule, Armstrong's space suit, and the bicycle he rode as a boy. Visitors are given a guided tour of the museum, which chronicles Armstrong's achievements up to and including the *Apollo 11* mission. When an occasional visitor asks what Armstrong has done since then, the guides have no answer.

Because of his reluctance to be in the public eye, people have called him distant, aloof, and cold. On the other hand, his friends say he is warm, loyal, and witty.

Some people, like Julian Scheer, who was head of public affairs for NASA during the Apollo missions, say that what is really remarkable about Armstrong is that he has never changed. "Neil's the same sort of private person he always was," Scheer said. "He didn't cash in; he didn't seek celebrityhood. When you think of Neil Armstrong as a genuine American hero, there's no tarnish."[4]

On a clear night, Armstrong may still pause to gaze at the moon, but now he sees it in a different way. "I used to see a flat disk," he said. "Now I see it as places I've been."[5]

Chronology

1930—Born in Wapakoneta, Ohio, on August 5.

1947—Graduates from Blume High School; enrolls at Purdue University on a Navy scholarship.

1949—Called to active duty by the United States Navy.

1951—Sent to Korea as a fighter pilot.

1952—Receives honorable discharge from the Navy; returns to Purdue University.

1955—Earns a B.S. degree in aeronautical engineering from Purdue University; becomes a civilian test pilot at Edwards Air Force Base near Los Angeles, California.

1956—Marries Janet Shearon on January 28.

1957—Son Eric (Ricky) is born.

1959—Daughter Karen is born.

1962—Daughter Karen dies; Armstrong chosen to be an astronaut; receives the Octave Chanute Award from the Institute of Aerospace Sciences.

1963—Son Mark is born.

1966—Commander of *Gemini 8,* his first space flight; receives NASA's Exceptional Service Medal.

1969—Becomes the first man to walk on the moon on July 20 during the *Apollo 11* mission; receives the Presidential Medal of Freedom.

1970—Earns a master's degree in aeronautical engineering from the University of Southern California.

1971—Resigns from NASA; becomes a professor at the University of Cincinnati; buys a farm near Lebanon, Ohio.

1978—Receives the Congressional Space Medal of Honor.

1979—Sets an altitude record for business jets at 51,000 feet; resigns from the University of Cincinnati; becomes chairman of the board for the Cardwell International Corporation in Lebanon, Ohio.

1982—Named chairman of Computing Technologies for Aviation, Inc. (CTA).

1984—Appointed to the National Commission on Space (NCOS).

1986—Serves on the Rogers Commission investigating the space shuttle *Challenger* accident.

1994—Divorced from wife Janet and remarries.

1996—Continues to serve on the boards of various corporations.

Chapter Notes

Chapter 1

1. *Apollo 11*, Technical Air-to-Ground Voice Transcription, Manned Spacecraft Center, Houston, Texas, July 1969. All in-flight communications that follow come from this source.

2. Alan Shepard and Deke Slayton, *Moon Shot: The Inside Story of America's Race to the Moon* (Atlanta: Turner Publishing, 1994), p. 22.

3. Buzz Aldrin and Malcolm McConnell, *Men From Earth* (New York: Bantam Books, 1989), pp. 238–239.

Chapter 2

1. Lawrence Mosher, "Neil Armstrong: From the Start He Aimed for the Moon," *National Observer*, July 7, 1969.

2. William K. Stevens, "The Crew: What Kind of Men Are They?" *The New York Times*, July 17, 1969, p. 31.

3. "Gemini 8 Astronauts Forced Down in Western Pacific After First Docking in Space," *The New York Times*, March 17, 1966, p. 20.

4. Steve Drake, "'Couldn't Be Prouder,' Says Doctor: Ex-scout Mate Recalls Neil," *Wapakoneta Daily News*, July 19, 1969.

5. "Astronaut's Home Town Swept By 'Moon Craze,'" *Post Standard* (Syracuse, N.Y.), July 4, 1969.

6. Ibid.

7. Dallas Boothe, "Neil Dreamed of Landing on Moon Someday: Jacob Zint, Brading, Crites Remember Him," *Wapakoneta Daily News*, June 27, 1969.

8. Charles Babcock, "Moon Was a Dream to Shy Armstrong," *Journal Herald* (Dayton, Ohio), July 11, 1969, p. 14.

9. Mosher.

10. Neil Armstrong, Michael Collins, and Edwin E. Aldrin, Jr., *First on the Moon: A Voyage with Neil Armstrong, Michael Collins, [and] Edwin E. Aldrin, Jr.* (Boston: Little, Brown, 1970), p. 114.

11. Babcock, p. 14.

12. Mosher.

13. Bob McKay, "An Ordinary Man," *Ohio Magazine*, April 1984, p. 26.

Chapter 3

1. Recollections written by Viola Armstrong to Dora Jane Hamblin. From the Dora Janc Hamblin papers available at the Iowa Women's Archives in the University of Iowa Libraries.

2. Neil Armstrong, Michael Collins, and Edwin E. Aldrin, Jr., *First on the Moon: A Voyage with Neil Armstrong, Michael Collins, [and] Edwin E. Aldrin, Jr.* (Boston: Little, Brown, 1970), p.115.

3. Lawrence Mosher, "Neil Armstrong: From the Start He Aimed for the Moon," *National Observer*, July 7, 1969.

4. Armstrong, Collins, and Aldrin, Jr., p. 19.

5. Ibid., p. 116.

6. William Furlong, "Bluntly, He Places Ideas Above People," *Lima News* (Lima, Ohio), June 13, 1969.

7. Neil Armstrong, "The Men Write About Themselves and What They Are Up to Now: 'I Decided to Get Aboard,'" *Life*, September 27, 1963, p. 84.

8. Armstrong, Collins, and Aldrin, Jr., p. 118.

9. "Transcript of Kennedy Address to Congress on U.S. Role in Struggle for Freedom," *The New York Times*, May 26, 1961, p. 12.

Chapter 4

1. Neil Armstrong, "The Men Write About Themselves and What They Are Up to Now: 'I Decided to Get Aboard,'" *Life*, September 27, 1963, p. 84.

2. Ibid.

3. Ibid.

Chapter 5

1.Neil Armstrong, "Flying the Mission Make-Believe," *Life*, September 25, 1964, p. 140.

2. Al Kattman, "Wapak Awaits Neil's Space Adventure: Astronaut's Parents Worry, Leave for Launch Site," *Lima News* (Lima, Ohio), March 6, 1966, p. A12.

3. Ibid.

4. *Gemini VIII*, Voice Communications (Air-to-Ground, Ground-to-Air, and On-Board Transcription), Manned Spacecraft Center, Houston, Texas, March 18, 1966. All in-flight communications that follow come from this source.

Chapter 6

1. "At 'The Limit,' Man Prevails," *Newsweek*, March 28, 1966, p. 62.

2. "Text of NASA's Statement on the Failure of Gemini 8," *The New York Times*, March 20, 1966, p. 83.

Chapter 7

1. Neil Armstrong, Michael Collins, and Edwin E. Aldrin, Jr., *First on the Moon: A Voyage with Neil Armstrong, Michael Collins, [and] Edwin E. Aldrin, Jr.* (Boston: Little, Brown, 1970), p. 27.

2. Buzz Aldrin and Malcolm McConnell, *Men From Earth* (New York: Bantam Books, 1989), p. 215.

3. Michael Collins, *Carrying the Fire: An Astronaut's Journeys* (New York: Farrar, Straus & Giroux, 1974), p. 347.

4. Ibid., p. 434.

5. William Furlong, "Bluntly, He Places Ideas Above People," *Lima News* (Lima, Ohio), June 13, 1969.

6. "Armstrong Aimed at Moon Walk," *Journal Herald*, July 10, 1969.

7. Neal Stanford, "Pride in Achievement: NASA Hails Apollo Program as 'Triumph of the Squares,'" *Christian Science Monitor*, July 16, 1969.

8. Ibid.

9. Armstrong, Collins, and Aldrin, Jr., p. 46.

10. Collins, p. 344.

11. Audio Highlights Tape from NASA, "Apollo 11 Highlights—Lunar Landing," Lion Recording Studios.

12. Ibid.

13. Ibid.

Chapter 8

1. *Apollo 11*, Technical Air-to-Ground Voice Transcription, Manned Spacecraft Center, Houston, Texas, July 1969.

2. Ibid.

3. Audio Highlights Tape from NASA, "Apollo 11 Highlights—Lunar Landing," Lion Recording Studios.

4. "Harrowing Moments Led to First Walk on Moon," *Lima News* (Lima, Ohio), July 16, 1989.

5. *Apollo 11*, Technical Air-to-Ground Voice Transcription.

6. Log of Apollo 11, Manned Spacecraft Center, Houston, Texas, July 1969.

7. *Apollo 11*, Technical Air-to-Ground Voice Transcription.

8. Ibid.

9. Ibid.

10. Ibid.

11. Ibid.

12. Ibid.

13. Audio Highlights Tape.

14. *Apollo 11*, Technical Air-to-Ground Voice Transcription.

15. Ibid.

16. Ibid.

17. Ibid.

18. Audio Highlights Tape.

19. Ibid.

20. Ibid.

Chapter 9

1. "Greatest Week in the History of the World Since the Creation," *U.S. News & World Report*, August 4, 1969, p. 4.

2. "Armstrong's Parents on Cloud 9 After Walk," *Lima News* (Lima, Ohio), July 20, 1989.

3. "Armstrong Aimed at Moon Walk," *Journal Herald*, July 10, 1969.

4. Ira Berkow, "Cincinnati's Invisible Hero," *The Cincinnati Post*, January 17, 1976.

5. Al Salvato, "In Search of the Man on the Moon," *The Cincinnati Post*, July 16, 1994, p. 1A.

6. Tim Graham, "A Rare Talk with the Man from the Moon," *The Cincinnati Post*, March 3, 1979, p. 8.

7. Dora Jane Hamblin, "Neil Armstrong Refuses to 'Waste Any Heartbeats,'" *Life*, July 4, 1969, p. 21.

8. Berkow.

9. Ibid.

10. Graham.

Chapter 10

1. Matthew Purdy, "In Rural Ohio, Armstrong Quietly Lives on His Own Dark Side of the Moon," *The New York Times*, July 20, 1994, p. A14.

2. Ibid.

3. Jim Bebbington, "Armstrong Remembers Landing Delights Auglaize Show Crowd," *Dayton Daily News*, July 18, 1994.

4. John Noble Wilford, "Three Voyages to the Moon: Life After Making History on TV," *The New York Times*, July 17, 1994, Sec. 1, p. 21.

5. Marilyn Dillon, "Moon Walk Remains a Thrill," *Cincinnati Enquirer*, June 12, 1979, p. 1A.

Further Reading

Aldrin, Buzz, and Malcolm McConnell. *Men From Earth: An Apollo Astronaut's Exciting Account of America's Space Program.* New York: Bantam Books, 1989.

Armstrong, Neil, Michael Collins, and Edwin E. Aldrin, Jr. *First on the Moon: A Voyage with Neil Armstrong, Michael Collins [and] Edwin E. Aldrin, Jr.* Boston: Little, Brown, 1970.

Birmingham, Stephen. "Neil Armstrong Today: A Shy Hero Talks About Himself." *Ladies Home Journal,* August 1974, pp. 82–83 ff.

Bond, Peter. *Heroes in Space: From Gagarin to Challenger.* New York: Basil Blackwell, 1987.

Chaikin, Andrew. *A Man on the Moon: The Voyages of the Apollo Astronauts.* New York: Viking, 1994.

Collins, Michael. *Carrying the Fire: An Astronaut's Journey.* New York: Farrar, Straus & Giroux, 1974.

Hamblin, Dora Jane. "Neil Armstrong Refuses to 'Waste Any Heartbeats.'" *Life,* July 4, 1969, pp. 18–21.

Shepard, Alan, and Deke Slayton. *Moon Shot: The Inside Story of America's Race to the Moon.* Atlanta: Turner, 1994.

Stevens, William K. "The Crew: What Kind of Men Are They?" *The New York Times,* July 17, 1969, pp. 31 ff.

Index